# THE JEWEL TREASURY OF ADVICE
*A Hundred Teachings from the Heart*

# THE JEWEL TREASURY OF ADVICE
*A Hundred Teachings from the Heart*

*The Wisdom of*

## DRIKUNG BHANDE DHARMARADZA

*Translated from Tibetan by*

### KHENPO KÖNCHOG GYALTSHEN RINPOCHE

*Edited by*

#### RICK FINNEY

VAJRA PUBLICATIONS

9301 GAMBRILL PARK RD. • FREDERICK • MD •21701

ISBN 0-9655988-1-0

Vajra Publications
9301 Gambrill Park Road
Frederick, MD 21701


Printed in the United States of America
10 9 8 7 6 5 4 3 2 1

Cover photograph of Lord Jigten Sumgön:
Khenpo Könchog Gyaltshen Rinpoche
Cover and text design: Diane Spencer Hume

*We dedicate the merit of this publication
to the long life of all lamas and
to peace and well-being in the world.*

# CONTENTS

# FOREWORD

The author of this remarkable and inspiring text, Drikung Bhande Dharmaradza (1704–1754), was the reincarnation of the great Drikung Dharmakirti (1595–1659), the first of the Drikung Kyabgön Chungtsang Rinpoches. Revered for centuries as combined emanations of Manjushri and Guru Padmasambhava, these great lamas—together with the Drikung Kyabgön Chetsang Rinpoches—have held the throne of the Drikung Kagyu lineage from the seventeenth century up to the present day.

In these *Hundred Teachings From The Heart*, Dharmaradza maps out, in verse, the entire structure of the Buddhist path. The teachings given here are honest and direct, yet rich in metaphor, and cover topics ranging from the first contemplations on impermanence to how the disciplines and vows of the three yanas may be practiced without conflict or contradiction. The book's concluding section, "The Life of

Drikung Bhande Dharmaradza," was taken from *The Golden Rosary of the Drikung Kagyu*, a lineage history composed by the Fourth Drikung Kyabgön Chetsang Rinpoche, Tendzin Pemai Gyaltsen (1770–1826).

Many people reviewed the manuscript of this translation at various stages of its production and offered encouragement and advice. Particular thanks are due to Stephen Willing, Belle Waring, Janice D. Willis, and Jinpa Zangpo for their close reading of the text and for their helpful editorial suggestions. Thanks also go to Diane Hume for her generous donation of design and typesetting services, to Yvonne Lim for her help in publishing this text, to Judith Hitt for her dedicated service to the Drikung Kagyu Text Project, and to all the members and friends of the Tibetan Meditation Center and affiliated groups.

Read with an open mind, these verses can penetrate the veil of discursive thought, leading to ever deeper and more profound levels of meaning. Still, the deeper meaning may sometimes elude our understanding. Questions on any aspect of the Buddha's teachings should always be referred to a qualified lama.

Rick Finney
Gaithersburg, Maryland
January 1996

# INTRODUCTION

Generally speaking, all sentient beings inherently wish to experience peace and happiness and to gain freedom from suffering and unfavorable conditions. However, they must be able to recognize these things for what they are. Human life has this quality of intelligence. In fact, it brings with it every opportunity to gain freedom from all suffering and to accomplish full enlightenment. We should recognize the truth of this for ourselves and cultivate the confidence that we, too, can use this precious human life as a ship to cross the ocean of samsara.

The appearance of a Buddha in this world is rare. The taking of an interest in the Dharma is also rare. It is rare to obtain the precious human birth and to enjoy good health, and it is rare to find an opportunity to practice. If we do not make use of these circumstances now when we have them, how can we hope to ever find them again?

Although this precious human body is difficult to find and possesses all excellent qualities, it is impermanent. All composite phenomena are transitory, and this is particularly true of our human life. All the great enlightened masters and powerful rulers of nations who have ever lived have vanished without a trace. No matter how important we are to our family or society—no matter how much is left for us to learn or to do—when the time comes, we will have to face our death. Therefore, we should follow the example of Milarepa, who said:

> *Out of fear of death, I escaped to the mountains.*
> *Because of the uncertainty of the time of death,*
> *I persisently practiced the Dharma.*
> *I captured the fortress of the unchanging nature of mind.*
> *Now I am free from the fear of death.*

Since the sole purpose of our practice and study of Dharma is to bring peace—both for ourselves and for others—in this life, at the time of death, and in our future lives, we should observe the changing of the seasons, the change of day to night, and apply ourselves to practice in every moment.

All sentient beings exist from moment to moment in a state of suffering. Many, especially in the three lower realms, experience the suffering of physical and mental pain. Others, in more fortunate circumstances, experience the suffering of change when their temporary happiness and enjoyment give way to sorrow. Friends may become enemies. Food may turn into poison. We are disappointed when we don't get what we want, and we helplessly meet with what we would like to avoid.

These various sufferings are nothing more than the results that arise from our own nonvirtuous actions and thoughts, and so it is useless to struggle against them. In fact, we can learn to approach our suffering in a positive way. Suffering can remind us to be aware of our ongoing accumulation of causes and their inevitable effects, which we alone will have to experience. Suffering also undermines our arrogance, brings us down to earth, and inspires us to look for solutions. Because of our suffering, we can better understand others who are in pain. And when we become convinced of the inexorable quality of karmic causation, we will be effective and sincere in our resonsibility for ourselves and others.

Since all sentient beings exist within this state of suffering, it can be helpful to see them as our parents, friends, or children and to cultivate the same loving-kindness and compassion toward them that we experience toward our own parents, friends, and children of this life. Compassion, in particular, is one of the principal antidotes to the afflicting emotions, especially anger and resentment. It extends itself to all beings, wishing to free them from their suffering, and brings with it a deep sense of space and relaxation. Those who possess compassion become attractive to others and are respected by everyone. Compassion opens our heart.

When we have some experience of this genuine loving-kindness and compassion, we can begin to cultivate bodhicitta, the fully awakened mind that wishes to achieve buddhahood for the benefit of all sentient beings. As the best path to the purification of the afflicting emotions and subtle obscurations and to the perfection of wisdom-awareness, bodhicitta is the ultimate source of all benefit, peace, and happiness. Bodhicitta is the universal mind that embraces every sentient being from the heart. Mental acuity, confidence, and courage: all these excellent qualities and others arise from the practice of bodhicitta.

There are two kinds of bodhicitta, that concerned with aspiration and that concerned with activity. The bodhicitta of aspiration is the altruistic thought to obtain buddhahood for the benefit of others. This can be compared to the wish to go to a certain place. The bodhicitta of activity puts the bodhicitta of aspiration into effect, in the same way that one would prepare for and then set out on a journey. This includes all practice and study undertaken to train the mind, including the disciplines of the six paramitas.

The first of these paramitas, generosity, cuts through our selfishness. The second, morality and ethics, disciplines our body, speech, and mind so that we can avoid negative actions and cultivate virtue. The third, patience, helps us to attain fearlessness and confidence. The fourth, perseverance, channels the energy and strength we need to gather the two accumulations of merit and wisdom. The fifth, meditative concentration, is the method of abiding in one-pointed calm, free from distractions and mental obscurations. The sixth, wisdom-awareness, penetrates the all-pervading nature of the mind and dispels all delusions; this is the special insight that transcends the duality of grasping and fixation.

Bodhicitta is the backbone of the Buddhadharma. Without it, there is no way to obtain buddhahood or to benefit countless numbers of beings; yet, if one possesses bodhicitta, one helplessly becomes a buddha. Lord Jigten Sumgön said, "Buddhahood is the mental formation of bodhicitta." The cultivation of bodhicitta is thus one of the best methods to be free from all outer and inner obstacles and hindrances, both in our ordinary lives and on the path to enlightenment. Bodhicitta is the supreme wheel of protection.

Those who have this foundation of training in the causal vehicle and who have a good understanding of the general teachings of the Buddha can begin the practice of tantra. The word tantra itself means "continuity" and refers to the continuity of the unchanging nature of enlightened mind, the buddha nature. The practice of tantra is a powerful and direct method to awaken this luminous nature of mind. Especially through the ceremony of the four empowerments, one receives the potential to purify one's ordinary body and manifest the body of a deity, to purify ordinary speech and manifest wisdom-speech, to purify the obscurations of mind and realize wisdom-mind, and to purify the obscurations of duality and recognize the all-pervading nature of enlightenment. The Six Yogas of Naropa in particular—the practices of *tummo,* clear light, dream yoga, the illusory body, *phowa,* and *bardo*—contain the very essence of all the teachings of tantra. The proper accomplishment of these methods cuts through all samsaric delusion and allows the enlightened mind to manifest directly.

In order to study and practice this magnificent path—in order to be free from samsara and attain enlightenment—it is essential to have a fully qualified teacher. For example, if one were to try to cross the ocean in a ship with no captain, one would have no hope at all of reaching the opposite shore. In the same

way, one needs a qualified teacher to lead one safely
to one's goal, especially on the path of tantra. When
teachers themselves are confused, though, they will
not be able to properly guide their students. One may
practice guru yoga, seeing one's lama as the four kayas
of a buddha, but this is not just guru worship; rather,
it is the way to awaken the mind and receive the full
blessings of enlightenment. Lord Jigten Sumgön said:

> I, a yogin, realized the unity
>    of the guru, my own mind, and the Buddha.
> I have no need of superficial devotion.
> In noneffort, I, the yogin, am happy.
> This happy yogin experiences joy.
> This experience of joy is the guru's kindness.

Enlightenment is the all-pervading wisdom of emptiness, the unity of nonobjectified great compassion
and intrinsic awareness. All of samsara and nirvana is
"sealed" (mudra) by this nature, and there is nothing
"greater" (maha) than this. Therefore, it is called
mahamudra. When one realizes this nature, it is called
nirvana. When one fails to realize this, one wanders in
samsara. Nagarjuna said, "There is no difference between samsara and nirvana. When one realizes the
nature of samsara, that is called the attainment of
nirvana."

In order to practice mahamudra, one should first make effort to practice calm-abiding meditation through the method of watching the breath. First, sit in a comfortable seat and relax your mind. Then take a deep, full breath and exhale, expelling all tension. Then breathe naturally through your nostrils and, taking your breath as your object, rest your mind. When your mind wanders, simply bring it back to an awareness of the breath. In this way, tame your mind and stabilize it in one-pointed calm. Alternatively, visualize at your heart-center a blue-colored light about the size of a mustard seed and, taking that as your object, rest your mind. When thoughts arise, without chasing after them or pushing them away, let them dissolve into the blue light and let them rest.

This training dispels confusion and establishes the mind in clarity and peace, and on the basis of this stability—and through the pointing-out instructions— one realizes mahamudra, the all-pervading nature of the mind. At that time, all gross afflicting emotions are seen to be of the nature of emptiness. Then, there is nothing to accept and nothing to reject. Simply be aware of this unfabricated experience of things as they are. In the same way that space is primordially free from clouds, this nature is inexpressible in its vastness and profundity. This is what it is like when the mind is free from conceptual thoughts. This is total freedom.

# Introduction

Dedication is the method to fully establish the fruit of whatever practice one has done. One may have accumulated a great deal of merit, but if it has not been dedicated, its result may be wasted before it manifests. One's own virtue and the virtue of all others in the past, present, and future—along with the inherent virtue of buddha nature itself, which is possessed by everyone—should be dedicated to the attainment of complete enlightenment for oneself and all sentient beings. This method of dedication not only increases virtue's result, but, like a drop of water merging with the ocean, that virtue becomes inexhaustible until one attains complete buddhahood.

It is very important for every practitioner to attend to this simple yet effective method.

Khenpo Könchog Gyaltshen
Frederick, Maryland
September 1995

*The Jewel Treasury of Advice*

# The Jewel Treasury of Advice

*A Hundred Teachings from the Heart*

I give this advice as a reminder to myself.

With one-pointed mind, I supplicate the supreme,
    victorious Ratna Shri[1]
and the one who holds the name Bhadra,[2]
the embodiment of all refuges.
Please grant your blessings so that I may actualize
    the life of the lama.

I don't know much about the two ways of life[3]
and have not studied the various classes of knowledge,
so I am not qualified to write these words of advice.
But because you, my close attendant,
    have asked me so persistently,
I will briefly set down whatever comes to mind.

A body endowed with leisure and fortune[4]
is the supreme basis, which is difficult to find.

You have entered into the precious teachings
   of the Buddha
and have especially heard the Vajrayana Dharma.
So don't waste your human life.
Cherish your practice.

According to the teachings of cause and example
   and so forth,
leisure and fortune are difficult to find.
Even if one is born as a human,
vast regions remain without the Dharma.
Buddhas appear and teach the Dharma very rarely.
In particular, it is barely possible to hear
the teachings of secret mantra.
Life doesn't stand still for even a moment.
So think carefully, can you afford to waste
   this leisure and fortune?

The root of the Buddha's teachings is the morality
   of the vinaya.
Without this, even if you are called a practitioner,
you are still a samsaric person.
Therefore, guard your discipline
   as you would your eyes.

Desires are the hoard of nonvirtue.
Spirituality aside, even in the ordinary, worldly life

there are many who have lost life, wealth, and power.
Therefore, regard desire as an enemy.

Beer and the others in its group[5] are the source
   of all harm.
Liquor, even if you boil it,
still possesses great faults.
Gradually, come to regard even beer as a poison.

Also, wandering distractedly,
giving in to vanity and frivolity
and watching others dance and sing and so forth
are like the sounds that lure wild animals to their
   death.
These increase desire and the deceptiveness of samsara.
Therefore, avoid them.

Through wearing robes, one cultivates a virtuous
   mind.
Wearing lay dress and weapons is a cause of the mind
   of nonvirtue.
In particular, religious dress inspires
   and reminds one of renunciation.
It is a sign of the glory of the Victor's teachings.
Therefore, abandon meaningless dress.
Be an ornament to inspire those who have devotion.

Meaningless diversions and idle tales
are a cause of wasting one's life
　　and of obstructing the Mind of Dharma and so forth.
You should develop as much virtue as you can.
All wealth is like the honey of the bees.
It binds one to samsara and is freely taken by others.
Much is lost and wasted to no purpose.
Therefore it is important to take wealth's essence
by using it for the Dharma and by practicing generosity.

Ceaseless chatter is a source of faults
　　and is despised by others,
but if we are completely silent we cannot point the way.
Therefore, it is important to know when to speak.

Due to the degeneration of the times,
many of those friends who we have aided
　　will arise as enemies.
Provoked by advice, confidences, and so forth,
many will become argumentative and resentful.
There are many who mistake our help for harm.
Therefore, whatever benefit you provide
　　through the giving of wealth and so forth,
do it without expectation and with a noble mind.
The fruit of this will ripen without a doubt.
It is important to know when to offer heartfelt words.

Abandon that which harms yourself
　　and doesn't benefit others.
If you expect too much from your good deeds,
you will often be let down.
Keep this in your heart.

Some may have a good manner
　　but be like a poisonous snake.
The behavior of others may be unpleasant,
but they may have noble thoughts
and may perform many Dharma activities
　　and so forth.
Therefore, don't rely on first impressions.
Look closely at their character.

If you overreact with like or dislike
to small amounts of benefit or harm,
in the long run you won't know
　　who will help or harm you.
It is good to respond without much anger or delight.
Have noble thoughts.
Be even, like the strings of a guitar.

If someone speaks harsh words, try to see
　　if they are true.
Many are deceived, like the rabbit who heard "Chal."[6]

If someone depends on you from their heart,
it is important to treat them like yourself.
If you betray them, you will experience that result.
So be careful.

Knowing the various aspects
of ritual, dance, and melody and so forth[7]
is a source of upliftment.[8]
It is important to make effort in this.
But if you are bound by jealousy and pride,
the result of your practice will be birth in lower realms.
Therefore, establish the true meaning
    of this and future lives
by having noble thoughts
and by generating loving-kindness.

You may think that small actions of virtue
    and nonvirtue
may not help or harm.
But small karma gives rise to great results.
So be careful even in little things.

Saying or doing whatever comes to mind
is the storehouse of all nonvirtue.
Investigate before you act.
Until you gain the fruit of what you do,
it is important to continue.

If you are too direct, you will make enemies.
Improper behavior ripens heavy karma.
Getting along with everyone is superficial.
Not getting along with everyone is worse.
Therefore, it is important to be skillful
    in various methods
and to be free from deceit, cunning, and
    nonvirtuous mind.

Bodhicitta is the source of all bodhisattvas,
and all Dharma is only for the benefit of others.
Especially on the path of attaining buddhahood
    in one life,
it is essential to practice the teachings
of arising and completion of secret mantra.

In this degenerate time, many rely on ghosts.
The worship of *te-rang*[9] as deities is like death
    at the edge of a knife.
It creates mischief and takes one's life for no purpose.
Therefore, to the unfailing Three Jewels,
go for refuge from the bottom of your heart.

Some do not fully trust the benefits
of the Buddha's speech, the holy Dharma.
Instead, they put their faith in *mo* and *bön*.[10]

This kind of wrong view is a cause
    for rebirth in the hells.
The results of obscurations of wealth
    and mistaken behavior and so forth
may not appear immediately, but will ripen
    without a doubt.
So fully trust.

The root of attainments is the vajra master.
Developing faith in all his activities,
holding his instructions as valid,
and respectfully serving and attending him
    without hypocrisy
is the root of all Dharma.[11]
But those who think that samaya is like an egg[12]
    deceive themselves.
This is my heart's advice.

Ordinary people can't keep the discipline
    of the shravakas,
yet many think that the vows of secret mantra,
    the discipline of maha aryas, are easier to keep.
Even though the activities of union and liberating[13]
    and so forth are stated in the tantras,
these are the deeds only of those on pure bhumis.
In the name of secret mantra, some take women,

drink, wear strange clothes,
and act like madmen and so forth.
If in this way one deceives oneself,
one will become stuck in the mud of samsara
and then fall to the depths of hell.

One cannot accomplish buddhahood
    without holding all three vows.
If you observe purely the discipline of the vinaya,
bind all you do to bodhicitta,
and practice the arising and completion stages
    of secret mantra,
it will not be difficult to gain the fruit
    of the three kayas.

Thus, I have briefly presented this general advice.
Now, for those who wish to practice the holy Dharma
    from the depths of their heart,
I will explain these things by means of analogy.

Impermanence and death are like the spreading shadow
    of sunset at the mouth of a pass.
It approaches without stopping for even an instant.
Apart from Dharma, nothing will help.
This is my heart's advice.[14]

The joy and happiness of this life are like a dream
   and illusion.
We are left with nothing at the time of death.
Practice the holy Dharma without distraction.
This is my heart's advice.

The eight worldly concerns are like a snare.
Exhausted by meaningless effort, we end our lives
   in dissatisfaction.
Meditate well on renunciation.
This is my heart's advice.

The appearance of happiness is like burning ash.[15]
Unaware of this, we cannot reach the final goal.
Make effort to generate revulsion.[16]
This is my heart's advice.

Activities done only for this life
   are like a moth drawn into a flame.
Deceiving oneself in this way is only a cause
   of suffering.
Abandon attachment to samsara.
This is my heart's advice.

The activities of samsara are like ripples of water.
Before they cease, our lives come to an end.

Quickly give up concern for them.
This is my heart's advice.

Relatives and friends can be like prison guards.
There are many who obstruct those who wish to
practice the holy Dharma from the depths of their
     heart.
Cut the mental bonds of clinging.
This is my heart's advice.

Sweethearts can be like butchers holding knives.
Even if we benefit them, they respond to our kindness
     with harm.
Abandon attachment to everyone.
This is my heart's advice.

The activities of this degenerate age
are like a madman's performance of dance.
No matter what we do,
there is no way to please others.
Think about what is essential.
This is my heart's advice.

Almost all speech is like the startling sound of "Chal."
It has no essence and results in many deceptions.
Investigate carefully.
This is my heart's advice.

All desires are like poisonous food.
They are the cause of nonvirtue and cut the root
    of liberation.
Apply vigilance without distraction.
This is my heart's advice.

The results of virtue and nonvirtue
    are like the shadows of flying birds.[17]
We may not see them now, but they will appear
    at the time of death.
Make effort to abandon nonvirtue and to accomplish
    wholesome deeds.
This is my heart's advice.

The accumulation of wealth
is like bees gathering honey.
We are bound by it, and it is freely taken by others.
Therefore, accumulate merit through the practice
    of generosity.
This is my heart's advice.

Much of what we hope for and rely on is like a mirage.
It will deceive and upset you when you need it most.
Therefore, direct your mind toward the Dharma.
This is my heart's advice.

Even this cherished body is like an autumn flower.
In an instant, it is destroyed by
the frost of impermanence.
Therefore, without wasting time, contemplate death.
This is my heart's advice.

Sense objects are like filthy muck.
They have no essence, not even in their smallest part.
Therefore, you should generate
revulsion and contentment.[18]
This is my heart's advice.

Birth, old age, sickness, and death
are like fish struggling on hot sand.
Their fierce torment and suffering are intolerable.
Apart from Dharma, nothing will help.
This is my heart's advice.

One's consciousness in the bardo
    is like a feather blown by the wind.
Powerless, it is blown by the winds of karma
    and led by the Lord of Death.
Apart from the Three Jewels, there is no refuge.
This is my heart's advice.

The three lower realms are like an iron house
    with no door.
There, one is tormented by suffering
    and has no chance for liberation.
Therefore, attend closely to cause and result.
This is my heart's advice.

The bliss of higher realms is like poisonous food.
It has only the appearance of happiness
    and is only a cause of suffering.
Samsara has no essence.
This is my heart's advice.

Thus, the suffering of samsara is like a prison.
There is no chance for happiness or freedom there.
Therefore, generate pity and revulsion.
This is my heart's advice.

Offering-wealth, meat, and the wealth of sinful persons
    are like burning ash.[19]
They carry heavy sin and obstruction
and obscure all one's virtuous qualities.
Therefore, make effort in purifying meditation
    and recitation.
This is my heart's advice.

Heartfelt recollection of the Dharma
is like one's hair, caught on fire.
Nothing is as important as that.
Therefore, don't be lazy or attached to pleasure.
This is my heart's advice.

Renunciation and the mind that abandons negativity
are like a captain piloting a ship.
Freedom from samsara depends upon them.
Therefore, always think on this without distraction.
This is my heart's advice.

Obtaining a life of leisure and endowments
is like arriving at a continent of jewels.
Whether we attain liberation or not is up to us.
Be sure, therefore, not to leave empty-handed.
This is my heart's advice.

Knowingly doing wrong is like a madman
taking his own life.
One only destroys oneself in this way.
Remember this again and again.
This is my heart's advice.

The spiritual friend is like a guide on the path.
He protects one from the lower realms
    and leads one to liberation.

Attend him respectfully with body, speech, and mind.
This is my heart's advice.

The holy Dharma that he teaches is like the nectar
   of immortality.
It dispels all faults and possesses all good qualities
   without exception.
Make offerings to him of the three ways of pleasing.
This is my heart's advice.

Not taking the teachings to heart through practice
is like the sound of an echo.
It is empty and without meaning.
Therefore, apply your mind to the Dharma.
This is my heart's advice.

The four preliminaries are like the foundation
   of a building.
Without them, nothing can be perfected.
Therefore, cherish persistent recollection.
This is my heart's advice.

The supreme place of solitude is like a
   well-guarded fort.
The eight worldly concerns are the cause of
   wandering mind.

Therefore, keep to the mountains and retreat.
This is my heart's advice.

The precious teachings of the Drikung Kagyu,
which are like the treasury of a king,
lack nothing of the holy Dharma.
There is no need to depend on anything else.
This is my heart's advice.

The Three Jewels are like the sphere of the sun.
Their compassion is impartial and unfailing.
Take refuge from the bottom of your heart.
This is my heart's advice.

The stain of bad deeds and obscurations
    is like mud covering a jewel.
Even though the alaya is pure,
    it cannot manifest the qualities.[20]
The confession of four powers is essential.
This is my heart's advice.

One who gathers the two accumulations
    is like a wise investor.
Though he enjoys his wealth, it is never exhausted.
Therefore, apply yourself to virtuous deeds.
This is my heart's advice.

Mahayana dedication is like a well-guarded treasure.
It bears fruit each day until enlightenment is won.
It accomplishes the benefit of oneself and others.
This is my heart's advice.

The pratimoksha vow is like the Holder of Jewels.[21]
Without depending on this, there is no holy Dharma.
It is the foundation of everything.
This is my heart's advice.

Pure morality is like a precious shrine,
    imbued with sacred power.[22]
It is an object of prostrations for all beings,
    including the gods.
One should guard the three trainings
    as one guards one's eyes.
This is my heart's advice.

Immorality's effects are unclean, like a corpse.
They arouse the concern of holy persons
    and destroy the root of virtue.
Those who violate morality become
    an object of scorn.
This is my heart's advice.

Loving-kindness is like a warrior victorious in battle.
In an instant, it annihilates all the hordes of maras
    without exception.
Meditate on all beings as your parents.
This is my heart's advice.

Supreme compassion is like a skillful mother
    nurturing her child.
Abandoning comfort, it engages in
    the benefit of others.
Therefore, generate the courage of the
    altruistic thought.
This is my heart's advice.

The supreme mind of bodhicitta is like an unspoiled
    seed.
Without it, it is impossible to achieve
    perfect enlightenment.
Therefore, cherish the cultivation of the
    mind of mahayana.
This is my heart's advice.

Aspiration bodhicitta is like a traveler setting out
    on a journey.
Before long, he will arrive at buddhahood.
Therefore, make a pure aspiration.
This is my heart's advice.

The bodhicitta of activity is like a well-built channel.
Through that, one can—without care—perfect
   the two accumulations.
Merit will continually arise.
This is my heart's advice.

The giving of generosity, free from attachment,
is like a farmer sowing seeds.
It accomplishes our wishes and intentions
   without waste.
Discover the essence of your wealth.
This is my heart's advice.

The three kinds of morality are like a warrior's sword.
They cut the bonds of the obscuring emotions.
You should possess recollection, decorum,
   awareness, and consideration.
This is my heart's advice.

The armor of patience is like a protective suit.
It cannot be pierced by anger,
   and it will increase all one's virtuous qualities.
Through patience, one will attain a body
   adorned by the major and minor marks.[23]
This is my heart's advice.

The three kinds of perseverance are like a steed
  encouraged by the whip.
They are the supreme method to
perfect the holy Dharma
and to quickly free oneself from samsara.
This is my heart's advice.

Meditative equipoise is like a glorious palace.
One can abide there in peace and joy
and can rest there from samsara.
Practice samadhi without wandering mind.
This is my heart's advice.

Discriminating awareness is like a clear-seeing eye.
It can distinguish all dharmas without mistake.
It is the lamp on the path to liberation.
This is my heart's advice.

The supreme vajra vehicle is like the lord of elephants.
In an instant, without difficulty, it brings
  complete enlightenment.
It is the essence of the teachings.
This is my heart's advice.

The root lama is like a wish-fulfilling jewel.
He is the source of all good qualities.

Therefore, attend him with flawless respect.
This is my heart's advice.

Faultless devotion is like a well-plowed field.
It is the basis of all virtuous Dharma and prosperity.
Supplicate respectfully.
This is my heart's advice.

The lama's teachings are like a healing medicine.
His beneficial words are spoken for your sake.
Therefore, practice according to his instructions.
This is my heart's advice.

Making offerings of the three ways of pleasing
is like polishing a jewel.
It brings the rainfall of the supreme and common
    attainments.
The lama is the embodiment of all objects of refuge.
This is my heart's advice.

The samaya of the lama is like one's
    consciousness and life.
Abandoning it creates a corpse
    that cannot be revived.
One cannot do without it.
This is my heart's advice.

The ripening four empowerments
are like a stream of nectar.
They purify the four obscurations
   and plant the seeds of the four kayas.
They are the root of the path of mantra.
This is my heart's advice.

The generation stage is like the enthronement of a king.
Through that, one becomes lord of
all samsara and nirvana.
Therefore, abandon ordinary view.
This is my heart's advice.

The clarity of appearances is like Indra's bow.[24]
They are unmixed, vivid, complete, and insubstantial.
Abandon grasping at them.
This is my heart's advice.

Pure mindfulness is like a rosary of jewels.
It displays its various qualities one by one.
Each of them is needed.
This is my heart's advice.

Firm pride[25] is like a hero's jewel.
There is no need to search outside,
   as it is fully established from the beginning.

Understand your own true nature.
This is my heart's advice.

Vajra recitation is like a forest fire.
In an instant, it burns the two obscurations
    and all sickness, propensities, and *döns*.[26]
By means of it, one will quickly accomplish power.
This is my heart's advice.

The samaya of secret mantra is like a snake
    in a length of bamboo.[27]
If one keeps it, it brings complete enlightenment.
If one doesn't, it is a cause of the hells.
Therefore, protect it as you would your eyes.
This is my heart's advice.

The beneficial effects of magnificent blessings
are like a supreme and all-victorious medicine.
Because of them, the afflicting emotions
    are self-liberated,
and it is not difficult to gain complete enlightenment.
Secret mantra is the supreme, quick path.
This is my heart's advice.

View, action, and meditation are like
    the king of beasts.

Fearlessly, they overpower anything.
They form the pinnacle of the path.
This is my heart's advice.

Untimely yogic behavior is like a moth
    drawn into a flame.
Through this, one destroys oneself and falls
    to the vajra hell.
Therefore, avoid heedless, mad activity.
This is my heart's advice.

The all-creating mind is like a magician.
All the suffering and joy of samsara and nirvana
    arise from it.
Hold well the real meaning of the mind.
This is my heart's advice.

The completion stage is like a reflection
    in a mirror.
It is inexpressible and is free from the elaborations
    of existence or nonexistence.
It is a matter of self-awareness.
This is my heart's advice.

Keeping to one's practice is like enjoying
    one's own wealth.

It doesn't come from anyone else and is spontaneously
   established by oneself.
Guard your mind.
This is my heart's advice.

Giving up concern for this life
   is like a merchant whose work is done.
There is no better method to perfect the holy Dharma.
It is the king of actions.
This is my heart's advice.

Calm abiding is like a lamp unmoved by the wind.
Although the six objects are clearly present,
they are free from grasping by the mind.
Don't allow awareness to sink.
This is my heart's advice.

Panoramic awareness is like a calm, clear ocean.
In clarity and joy, sustain the recognition
   of movement and abiding.
Cut to the root of mind-as-such.[28]
This is my heart's advice.

Establishing the appearance of the mind
is like a thief in an empty house.
It is beyond color, form, shape, and characteristics.

There is no searcher and no object of a search.
This is my heart's advice.

Mind and conceptual thought are like water and ice.
They have always been inseparable,
yet cannot be said to be one thing or two.
This is my heart's advice.

The inseparability of appearance and mind
   is like last night's dream.
It possesses the four characteristics
   and is the union of appearance and emptiness.
It cannot be said to be one thing or two.
This is my heart's advice.

Coemergent mind-as-such is like an ocean wave.
Although discursive thought is settled,
the six objects are clearly present.
Clarity and emptiness are inseparable.
This is my heart's advice.

Ordinary mind is like the center of the sky.
It is untouched by thoughts of the three times,
and its mode of being is uncreated awareness.
This is my heart's advice.

Unbroken practice is like a watchful guard.
It is simply unscattered
    and is free from accepting or rejecting.
There is no duality of things to be abandoned
    and their antidotes.
This is my heart's advice.

Bringing everything to the path is like the medicine
    of the Youthful Healer.[29]
Even harmful beings do not exist
apart from one's mind.
Release, without grasping, whatever arises.
This is my heart's advice.

Attachment to calm abiding is like the frozen surface
    of a lake.
It is dull and undiscriminating mind.
It leads to the error of the formless realm.[30]
This is my heart's advice.

Grasping at the duality of things to be abandoned
    and their antidotes
is like a man with faulty vision.
Not understanding the mode of being,
one holds one's own projections as the enemy.
Cherish nonscattering and nongrasping mind.
This is my heart's advice.

An artificial view of emptiness
is like medicine becoming poison.
Disavowing cause and result
and saying there are no deities and no ghosts:
this is incurable.
This is my heart's advice.

Attachment to cessation[31] is like a raven's walk.
It cannot arrive at complete enlightenment.
It will fall to the vehicle of the shravakas.
This is my heart's advice.

Diverse experiences[32] are like a summer meadow.
There is nothing that will not arise,
such as clairvoyance and so forth.
Avoid pride and arrogance.
This is my heart's advice.

Self-grasping and wrong desire are like crops
    destroyed by a frost.
If the Dharma, which is meant to tame the mind,
    becomes a cause of arrogance,
the root of virtue is cut.
This is my heart's advice.

The premature benefit of beings is like a leader
    with no sight.

It is a cause of not helping others
and of suffering for oneself.
Make effort in loving-kindness, aspiration,
    and dedication.
This is my heart's advice.

Untimely signs and marks[33] are like sky-flowers.
Results without causes are deceptive.
These are obstacles of maras.
This is my heart's advice.

The wisdom blaze of tummo is like the cosmic fire.
Through tummo, even this ordinary body
can gain enlightenment in this life.
It is the center-beam of the path.
This is my heart's advice.

Luminosity, which dispels the darkness of ignorance,
is like a brilliant light.
It dispels the obstructions of the afflicting emotions
and brings realization of the freshness
    of self-awareness.
It is the essence of the path.
This is my heart's advice.

The manifestations and transformations
    of dream practice

are like a steed being trained in its skill.
Through this, one masters manifestation
    and transformation.
It blends the appearance of day and night.
It is the measure of the path.
This is my heart's advice.

The instruction of the illusory body
is like a reflection of the moon in water.
It destroys attachment to ordinary appearance,
the eight worldly concerns, and self-grasping.
It is the foundation of the path.
This is my heart's advice.

Phowa is like a giant garuda flying in the sky.
In an instant, it arrives at the pure land.
It is the messenger of the path.
This is my heart's advice.

The practice of bardo is like traveling a familiar road.
Free from fear, one recognizes confusion
    as one's own projection.
It is the receptionist of the path.
This is my heart's advice.

The profound path of the six Dharmas
is like a treasury of jewels.

It contains all essentials of the classes of tantra.
It is the supreme instruction.
This is my heart's advice.

The three vows are like a carpenter's tools.
Without all three together,
    one cannot achieve perfect enlightenment.
Therefore, one should know how to keep them
    without contradiction.
This is my heart's advice.

Literal interpretation is like a physician
    with little knowledge.
Without agreement, one meaning may help,
    another may harm.
Therefore, one should understand the intention
    of the Kagyus.
This is my heart's advice.

The essential point of the three vows
is like a chariot's wheel.
Behaving like a shravaka, practicing
    secret mantra, and holding to bodhicitta
accomplish the goal.
This is my heart's advice.

The ten bhumis and five paths
  are like climbing a staircase.
Because of complete causes and conditions,
one can gradually progress.
One should maintain the activity of a bodhisattva.
This is my heart's advice.

The fruit of perfection is like a universal king.
It is without equal and fulfills all wishes.
It is completely free from hope and fear.
This is my heart's advice.

The dharmakaya, which has seven characteristics,
  is like space.
It is free from grasping and fixation
and from the elaborations of face, hands,
  and attributes.
It is beyond being an object of seeing or hearing.
This is my heart's advice.

The two kinds of form body are like the mandala
  of the sun and moon.
Even though they are without conceptual thought,
they appear according to the needs of beings.
They are the manifestation of compassion.
This is my heart's advice.

Uninterrupted compassion is like a river.
It doesn't tire or become discouraged.
It is equal to the limits of samsara.
This is my heart's advice.

This advice is like a treasury of jewels.
It lacks nothing for those who take the holy Dharma
  to their heart.
Practice it accordingly.
This is my heart's advice.

Thus, this heart advice is given as a series of analogies. Because they are analogies, they are not ultimately real, but if there were no similarity they could not be given as examples.[34] In particular, the profound path, the completion stage, and the three kayas and so forth cannot be defined by analogy. Yet, to further partial understanding, these analogies are given.

Alas! These days, some who pretend to be practitioners achieve a few of the experiences of calm-abiding and so forth and have some experience of the practice of inner channels. Possessing clairvoyance and so forth, they are deceived by maras. Because of this, they arrogantly believe they have achieved the dharmakaya.

Some think that the purpose of tummo is warmth. If this were true, even fire, clothing, and the sun could fulfill tummo's purpose. But through the practice of tummo, one can obtain the seven characteristics in this life.

Some are confused by the words "clear light." They think it is like the radiance of the sun. When they gain some experience of shallow clear light, they think they have achieved the supreme clear light of deep sleep.

Without even understanding the recitation of the three syllables, some think they are tantrikas and disparage the vinaya. Some proclaim themselves as realized, but their five poisons are coarser than others'. In solitude, some behave improperly. Whatever they do, they excuse as the display of dharmata. They misbehave and disavow cause and result. All this is only a cause of great sorrow.

Therefore, if you wish to practice the holy Dharma from the depths of your heart, receive the nectar of the teachings from an authentic lama. Then go to a solitary place, far from the activities of this life. Further, do not engage in heedless behavior. Outwardly, do not transgress the vinaya. Give up expectations of clairvoyance and miracle power.

Revulsion is the foot, or protector, of meditation. Hold in your mind an awareness of impermanence and the sufferings of samsara. Contemplate the essenceless nature and join your life-span with accomplishment.

Devotion is the head, or catalyst, of meditation. Therefore, with devotion, see the lama as the Buddha in person and supplicate continuously with respect.

Mindfulness is a sentry, or the actual practice. Therefore, never be apart from recollection of the mode of being.

Compassion is the activity of meditation. For the benefit of beings, contemplate bodhicitta and say prayers and dedications.

If you have no realization of your own, superficially guiding others and performing ceremonies of protection and so forth are obstacles of maras. Therefore, give these up.

The armor of meditation is regard for oneself and others. Be your own judge and do not arouse the concern of the lama, the Three Jewels, or your spiritual friends.

Fully cut the rope of attachment to this life. Although the practice of winds and channels with consort is proclaimed, if there arises even one moment of ordinary view, one will fall to the howling or vajra hell. This is therefore the activity of those on pure bhumis, the eighth through the tenth. If performed by ordinary beings, the result of this practice of Dharma will be a rock to sink one to the depths of samsara. Camphor is a supreme medicine, but if it is used for treating chills, there can be no hope. It is important to practice according to one's own ability. Faultless practice brings the vision of one's own primordial face.

Thus, I have presented—as a garland of words and verses—this common advice, the series of a hundred heart-teachings with analogies, and, again, the essential points of the practice of holy Dharma.

Because I, the Drikung Bhande Dharmaradza—a follower of the Victorious Lord Ratna Shri—opened a little the lotus of my wisdom because of the radiant sun of the holy Dharma speech of the glorious lama Karma Bhadra, and because of my deep sorrow at the sufferings of samsara and my desire to practice one-pointedly the essential meaning of the path, and in order to remind myself of the Dharma, and at the request of my attendant Könchok Drakden, and also in order to benefit those who take the Dharma to their heart, this was written.

By this virtue, may all sentient beings attain the level of buddhahood. May I, also, abandon the confusion of distracting activities. In this way, may I perfect this practice and achieve the fruit of the three kayas in this life.

## MANGALA AYUR SIDDHI RASTU

(Translated from the Tibetan by Khenpo Könchog Gyaltshen Rinpoche with the assistance of Rick Finney.)

# THE LIFE OF
# DRIKUNG BHANDE DHARMARADZA

*You are the embodiment of the vajra dance,*
*the three secrets of the Three Jewels,*
*the inconceivable activity of holding*
*the Victor's teachings and liberating all beings.*
*Döndrub Chökyi Gyalpo, I supplicate you.*

Trinley Döndrub Chögyal (Dharmaradza),
the reincarnation of the great Drikung
Dharmakirti, was born on the morning of
the twenty-fifth day of the Moon Month of the Wood
Monkey Year (1704) in Jang. His father's name was
Dresay Ngödrup Tashi, and his mother's name was
Namjom. His birth was accompanied by many auspicious signs, and, on that same day, rainbows appeared
and flowers fell from the sky in the area of Drikung.

The omniscient Könchok Trinley Sangpo, the
second Drikung Kyabgön Chetsang, whose fame
pervades the three worlds, had meanwhile received a

clear and unobstructed vision of this event and had written down its details. Giving directions and advice to the *chöppön* Chöjor, the *tsorpön* Bukge, and two other monks, he sent them to find the *tulku*. These four traveled south to Jang and searched in many places. Then they came to Laphir, a place whose qualities and features matched those found in the description given by Könchok Trinley Sangpo. When the search party heard that a special child had been born to Ngödrup Tashi, they immediately went to investigate.

The child, who was still only a few months old, became delighted when he saw them, and the party realized that he was without a doubt the incarnation they were seeking. They then returned to make their report, and on the way they discussed the situation with Taksham Tertön, who confirmed the child's identity. Then they arrived in Drikung and recounted all that had happened to Könchok Trinley Sangpo. Könchok Trinley Sangpo confirmed that they had indeed found the tulku, and he gave them a statue of Amitayus—together with many offerings and blessing pills—and sent them back to Jang. Eventually, they arrived again in Laphir. On an auspicious day, they named the child Könchok Trinley Döndrub and presented him with the statue and other gifts and offered prayers for his long life.

Könchok Trinley Sangpo then sent a party of seven, including the lama Trinley Wangchuk and the *drönyer* Rinchen Urgyen, with a complete set of the *Kangyur* and vast riches to obtain the child. When they arrived in Laphir, they offered all this to the child's father, but the father refused to part with his son, and this delayed matters for a time. During this period, the entire group visited the Five Deities Temple in Gyaltang, Döndrub Ling monastery, and Kongtse Rawa.

After finally receiving the father's permission to take the child, they began, on the first day of the first month, the return journey to Central Tibet. Although the boy was only six years old, he already understood Tibetan perfectly and was able to speak about the Dharma. Marvelous visions of Guru Padmasambhava and other enlightened beings appeared to him on the way. He visited Chamdo and many places in Nangchen. As his predecessor, Dharmakirti, had predicted, he opened the secret place of Lawa Gangchik. He then traveled through Jang, Pangchik, Wanak Gön, and other places. Large parties were sent out from Drikung Thil and Yangrigar to receive him, and in their company he went to the palace of Trolung. Rainbows appeared, and flowers rained down from the sky.

On the third day of the ninth month, Hlotrul Chökyi Gyatso, the chief disciple of Könchok Trinley Sangpo, and the general secretary Namgyal Horpön Sönam Wangchuk, along with other senior lamas and leading figures, received the young incarnation at the Supreme Vajra Place of Saten, greeting him with banners, parasols, and music that seemed to rival the wealth of the gods. The two lamas [editor's note: Könchok Trinley Sangpo and Drikung Dharmaradza] then met like father and son, and soon afterward they proceeded to Jangchub Ling at Drikung Thil to perform the hair-cutting ceremony before the statue of the peerless Lord Jigten Sumgön, Ratna Shri, which is like a wish-fulfilling jewel. And to the young lama's name was now added the title Chökyi Gyalpo. Visiting the shrine of Serkhang Dzamling Gyen, the chapel of the protectors, and other temples, Chökyi Gyalpo made great offerings, and he also made vast offerings to the assembly of monks.

Chökyi Gyalpo then began his studies and quickly mastered all known systems of reading and writing. To his attendants, he recounted the story of how the Buddha in one of his previous lives as a bodhisattva had offered his body to a tigress, how he himself had stayed in his wisdom-body form on the Copper-colored Mountain, and how he had then come to be born to his mother, and all who heard him were amazed.

At the age of seven, Chökyi Gyalpo received pre-novice vows from Könchok Trinley Sangpo. Then, over time, he attended Hlotrul Chökyi Gyatso, Taklung Wojo Tulku, Pelri Tulku, and many other great beings and studied the profound teachings of Lord Jigten Sumgön, the Fivefold Profound Path of Mahamudra, and all the teachings of the earlier great masters. He received numerous teachings and empowerments: the Vajra Mala, the Seven Mandalas of Ngok; the three traditions of Chakrasamvara (those of Luipa, Nakpopa, and Drilbupa); and various empowerments of the Four-armed Mahakala. He also studied the teachings of the great treasure-revealers: Nyang, Sangye Lingpa, Karma Lingpa, Ratna Lingpa, Jatsönpa, and others. In this way, he received count-less teachings and empowerments from the ancient and new traditions. In addition, he memorized the ritual systems and styles of dance, drawing, and chant-ing of the Drikung Kagyu monasteries. He also stud-ied poetry and the astrological systems of India and China. He mastered all common knowledge to per-fection.

In the month of Saga Dawa in the Water Snake Year, the father and son went to Lhasa to see the Jowo

Shakya and to offer gold-leaf to that statue and others. Together, they made great offerings of butter lamps, scarves, and so forth and made prayers of vast aspiration. At that time, Chökyi Gyalpo made a second offering of hair to the regent of the Sixth Dalai Lama and received the name Könchok Döndrub Rinchen. From Lhasa, he traveled to Drikung Thil and Terdrom Tsokhang, where Yeshe Tsogyal had stayed for many years, practicing the Dharma. A five-colored rainbow, witnessed by everyone, greeted him on his arrival. He then went to Tsewa Saten, where he settled for a time. In the Horse Year, many people gathered at the monastery of Trolung to mark a change in the administration, and both father and son went there and gave many vast and profound teachings.

In the Wood Sheep Year, when he was twelve, Chökyi Gyalpo entered into retreat to perform the practices of various *yidam* deities. In the first month of the Fire Monkey Year, he undertook a retreat on Yamantaka and experienced all the traditional signs of accomplishment. On this occasion, Könchok Trinley Sangpo carved, from red and white sandalwood, images of the Sixteen Arhats and of the Buddha and the eight manifestations of Mahakala and so forth. Chökyi Gyalpo carved images of Yamantaka with his consort and retinue and of the peaceful and wrathful

Manjushri. All these were done in precise detail and were magnificently beautiful.

In the sixth month of that same year, Chökyi Gyalpo went on pilgrimage to Terdrom. If interdependence and auspiciousness had come together, his life-span would have increased to seventy-six years and he would have revealed *terma*. But his attendant, Gelong Do Dorje, created obstacles to his activities. It thus became inauspicious for him to visit the holy places of the ancient and new traditions, and he could not open new ones. He undertook a strict retreat of one week, and on the tenth day he conferred an empowerment of the peaceful Guru Rinpoche on a large gathering of people. He then returned to Tsewa.

In the Fire Bird Year, when he was fourteen, he took the vows of a novice monk with Könchok Trinley Sangpo acting as *khenpo* and Hlotrul Chökyi Gyatso acting as *loppön*. He then received, in their entirety, the empowerments and teachings of the Eight Herukas of the Nyang tradition in the midst of a large gathering. He also received the teachings and empowerments of Lama Gongdu, together with instructions on Dharma medicine practice. Soon after this, the Dzungar Mongols invaded Tibet, and Chökyi Gyalpo went to Lhasa. The Dzungars destroyed the monasteries of Dorje Drak, Mindröling, and Dranang, killing many

lamas and causing much turmoil. But through the
blessings and skill of the father and son, no harm came
to the Drikung Kagyu.

In the Earth Dog Year, Chökyi Gyalpo returned to
his monastery. Könchok Trinley Sangpo's health then
began to fail, and Chökyi Gyalpo remained in his
presence to guard him and pray for his long life. After
Könchok Trinley Sangpo passed away, Chökyi Gyalpo
took charge of his cremation and invited many great
lamas to gather and perform ceremonies, all of which
were successfully completed. In particular, Shabdrung
Chödrak of Lungkar came to offer condolences and to
help in whatever way he could. As an offering to
Chökyi Gyalpo, Shabdrung Chödrak presented him
with an image of a youthful Manjushri made of
*dzikyim*, which had been the special practice support
of Loppön Prabahasti, and with a cup made from the
skull of one who had been born a Brahmin for seven
consecutive lives. Both of these objects had been
revealed as terma by Chöje Lingpa.

During this time, in the dream state, Chökyi Gyalpo
had a vision of Könchok Trinley Sangpo, who trans-
mitted to him a full empowerment of the Eight Herukas.
This was a sign that he would later establish a tradition
of the great accomplishment ceremony of this practice. In that same year, on the twenty-third day of the
tenth month, at Layel Thang at Jangchub Ling, Chökyi

Gyalpo ascended the golden throne as the regent of Lord Jigten Sumgön. In the Earth Pig Year, he completed work on the silver stupa of Könchok Trinley Sangpo, and an assembly of monks consecrated this with the performance of a Chakrasamvara sadhana. He also raised a statue at Trolung which was consecrated in the same way. Then, in a dream, Könchok Trinley Sangpo appeared again in his wisdom body, and Chökyi Gyalpo asked if he had made any mistake in the construction of these supports. To Chökyi Gyalpo's relief, Könchok Trinley Sangpo assured him that all had been properly fulfilled.

With the Chödze of Depa Lumpa, Chökyi Gyalpo then studied the two systems of Sanskrit—Kalapa and Tsandrapa—and, just on hearing them presented, quickly understood them. To further fulfill the intentions of Könchok Trinley Sangpo, he established, in the Iron Bird Year at Yangrigar, the tradition of the great accomplishment ceremony of the deity Tsogu, which had been composed by Dharmakirti.

Then, to protect Tibet from the ravages of the Dzungars, the K'ang-hsi emperor came. Chökyi Gyalpo went to meet him at Tsar Gungthang, where the two honored each other with an exchange of gifts. Soon after, the reincarnation of the Sixth Dalai Lama arrived from Lithang, and Chökyi Gyalpo went to receive him at Radreng valley by way of Lungsho.

Chökyi Gyalpo and his entourage welcomed him
with great ceremony, and they then traveled together
through Phenyul to Lhasa, where Chökyi Gyalpo
made great offerings during the Dalai Lama's enthronement. He then returned to Drikung.

In the Iron Ox Year, Chökyi Gyalpo traveled through
Lhasa to Drepung to see the Dalai Lama and to make
long-life offerings and hold close and open discus-
sions. While in Lhasa, he met many Chinese, Mongo-
lians, and Tibetans whom he satisfied with teachings
according to their individual wishes. He then returned again to Drikung.

During the time of the Dzungar occupation, there
had been a break in the continuity of the reversal
ceremonies of Shinje and Sotor, and these had gradually almost been lost. In the Water Tiger Year, Chökyi
Gyalpo restored these ceremonies to their former
strength. At Yangrigar, monastic discipline had de-
clined. Because of his conviction that the root of the
Buddha's teachings is the vinaya—and especially because Lord Jigten Sumgön had praised moral ethics—
Chökyi Gyalpo tightened the discipline at Yangrigar,
using both peaceful and wrathful means, and he
encouraged the monks in their study, contemplation,
and meditation and in the path of the ten virtuous
activities. For the use of the monasteries, he gathered
images, different types of cymbals from Hor, bro-

cades, silks, and other precious materials. Each year, he made offerings of these in quantities and of a quality beyond the imagination of ordinary people. In the Wood Dragon Year, he commissioned thirty-nine *thangkas* depicting the holders of the Golden Lineage of the Drikung Kagyu, and he completed the construction of Dzongsar Tashi Tsuk, which had been begun by Dharmakirti. Then he conducted elaborate consecrations.

Although inauspicious circumstances had manifested before when he had visited Terdrom, a chance remained that he could open secret places, in particular the Urgyen Cave. But when he sent some monks to find a road to these sites, Gelong Dode said that there was no way to go, and this became an obstacle to their discovery. In the later part of that year, Chökyi Gyalpo went to Terdrom, visited most of the old and new holy places nearby, and performed many feast-offerings and said many prayers of pure aspiration. When he arrived at the top of one of the new holy places, a mountain, a rainbow appeared, and all who were present heard the sound of a drum being beaten in the Mahakala Cave. Chökyi Gyalpo himself received visions of Milarepa, Tara, Dzambhala, and other awakened beings, and he pointed out the many self-arisen images that had appeared in that holy place.

By stages, he traveled around the mountain and came to the glorious retreat place, Tsa-Uk. In the Dorje Lokar Cave, Lord Jigten Sumgön's footprints had, over time, become hidden by dirt, and people could not easily find them. Chökyi Gyalpo found them all and showed them to his companions. At Terdrom and at Tsa-Uk, he himself left handprints in the rock. At Lord Jigten Sumgön's former residence at Tsa-Uk, Chökyi Gyalpo's party performed a longevity practice in retreat.

In the Wood Snake Year, on the fourth day of the sixth month—the day when Lord Buddha taught the Four Noble Truths—Chökyi Gyalpo traveled north with a large entourage to Taklung, Yangpachen, and other holy places. At Dechen Chökyi Phodrang in Shang Takna, on the auspicious eighth day of the month of Saga Dawa, he received the vows of full ordination from Trewo Rinpoche, Jangchub Chökyi Nyingpo. The two lamas then exchanged empowerments. Chökyi Gyalpo then toured the great holy place of Saphu Lung and the retreat place of Tashak.

Even though the principal meditation practice of Lord Jigten Sumgön had been Chakrasamvara, the numbers of people performing this meditation had decreased since his time. Chökyi Gyalpo therefore composed an abbreviated text for this sadhana and reestablished its practice. During this period, Chökyi Gyalpo received limitless offerings, gave many teachings, and distributed wealth to satisfy the needy. In the autumn, he returned to Yangrigar in Drikung. There, he strengthened the three streams of practice and established the *sojong* of the fourteenth and fifteenth days.

In the Earth Monkey Year, when problems arose in U-Tsang, he quickly went to Kongpo but returned soon after. Könchok Trinley Sangpo's reincarnation was then born to the Orong family of Kongpo. Chökyi Gyalpo clearly perceived this, and he sent Gelong Chöjor to find the tulku. The child recognized without error, but Önpo Hla Sithar and Sölpön Leksang disputed the recognition, and many people became confused by maras. The matter was taken to court.

Because of a misinterpretation of a prophecy of the oracle of a Dharma protector, the son of Hlasi was mistakenly recognized as the tulku, and this resulted in great controversy. Because of this, Chökyi Gyalpo went to Lhasa to see the ruler to present his case, and he received permission to conduct an urn ceremony in front of the precious Jowo. The first name to emerge from the urn was that of the son of Orong, who was the unmistaken incarnation. The second name was that of a candidate in a distant place. The third name, that of the son of Hlasi, did not come out at all. Thus, all ended well.

Then, in order to revive and increase the tradition of secret mantra of the Ancient Translation School, and also—as a root cause for the happiness of the Tibetan people—to reverse the causes of war, Chökyi Gyalpo established the great accomplishment ceremony of Nyang's Kagye Deshek Dupa at Yangrigar. He assigned the responsibilities for mandala construction, mask-making, and the gathering of materials and compiled the necessary texts. In this way, he benefited the teachings of the Nyingma school.

Soon after this, the former abbot of Yangrigar, Gyalse Trinley Tsedak—along with many others—went to bring back the tulku of Könchok Trinley Sangpo, and in the ninth month of the Earth Bird Year they arrived without obstacle in Drikung. With great joy, the father and son met at Tsewa. Then, in front of the statue of Lord Jigten Sumgön at Drikung Thil, they performed the first hair-cutting ceremony. It was a common practice at that time for people to eat meat during religious ceremonies. Chökyi Gyalpo felt that this was improper, especially during the recitation of longevity prayers, and asked everyone to reduce their attachment to this custom. He then gave all the teachings and empowerments—common and uncommon—of the Drikung Kagyu to the young tulku. In addition, both father and son received many teachings and empowerments from Hlotrul Chökyi Gyatso.

Before the Dzungar occupation, Trolung monastery had successfully maintained the *torma*-throwing traditions of Kagye, Mahakala, Trochu, and Guru Drakpo. In the Wood Tiger Year, Chökyi Gyalpo appointed teachers to restore these traditions. In the same way that he had tightened discipline at Yangrigar, Chökyi Gyalpo then began to speak against the consumption of alcohol by monks, even though they argued that by boiling liquor they removed its bad effects. Even in the preparation of the nectar used for blessing tormas, because of a general decline of realization due to obscurations of conceptual thought, no one performed this system properly. Because Lord Jigten Sumgön had said that for those with realization there is no difference between water, beer, and milk, Chökyi Gyalpo established the use of milk, tea, or clean water for this purpose and taught that alcohol should not be used at all.

Chökyi Gyalpo performed many retreats on Yamantaka, Chakrasamvara, Kalachakra, Yangsab, and the Dharma protector Achi and accomplished all the signs and realizations described in those texts. Once, while doing a longevity practice in retreat, he had a vision of Guru Rinpoche and the Dharma King Trisong Detsen surrounded by a rainbow.

Every six years, there was a rotation of the administrators of Yangrigar and Drikung Thil. On these occasions, Chökyi Gyalpo would present to retreatants the profound teachings of Lord Jigten Sumgön, the Fivefold Profound Path of Mahamudra, the Six Yogas of Naropa, Dzokchen according to the Yangsab, and other instructions. As a result of his teaching, many practitioners were produced who gave up all attachment to this life—in particular Gampo Tulku, Kunzang Ngedön Wangpo; the omniscient Drukpa, Kagyu Trinley Shingta; Katok Rigdzin Tsewang Norbu; Pawo Dorje Tsuklak; and others. These great beings received empowerments and teachings of both the old and new schools from Chökyi Gyalpo on many occasions. In Do-Me Tongkhor, Sara Chöje made offerings of wealth to Chökyi Gyalpo that rivaled the riches of Vaishravana.

Chökyi Gyalpo once painted a thangka of the Kagye Dedu, including depictions of his own future lives as Peljung Atima and so forth. He also commissioned statues, made from red and white sandalwood, depicting the twelve deeds of the Buddha. The artisan, Lujin, began work on these but then passed away, and the work was discontinued.

At Laphir in Jang, Chökyi Gyalpo established a new monastery, Thubten Dargye Ling, which was still flourishing at the time that this account was written [editor's note: in the eighteenth or nineteenth century]. Then—in order to maintain the continuity of the Buddha's teachings and to provide a support for the gathering of the two accumulations—he decided to build a temple, complete with images and furnishings, at Trolung. On an auspicious day of an auspicious month in the Earth Horse Year, he conducted elaborate groundbreaking ceremonies, and he then quickly built a temple of two stories and twelve pillars. This was completed in the first month of the Earth Sheep Year, and in the Iron Monkey Year he finished work on the interior—including paintings and shrine-shelves—and brought many images that had previously had no home. In the Iron Bird Year, he invited many Tibetan and Nepalese artisans to build an Enlightenment Stupa and a Miracle Stupa to subjugate evil forces, along with a Harmonizing Stupa for the blessings of life. Each of these was one and a half stories tall, made from gold and silver, ornamented with precious jewels, and of beautiful form. They were placed in the Hlundrub Dorje chapel, where Chökyi Gyalpo consecrated them many times.

In the Water Dog Year, Chökyi Gyalpo invited more artisans—along with their leader, Dorshing, and including those who had previously built the stupas—to construct an image called Great Sage, Ornament of the Three Worlds, Shower of Blessings.

Together with its golden parasol and throne, this stood two stories tall. To build this amazing statue—the mere sight of which inspires pure devotion—Chökyi Gyalpo used more than three thousand gold pieces and six hundred horseloads of copper. It was located in the chapel called Mingyur Dorje Den and was consecrated many times with elaborate ceremony with the practices of Chakrasamvara, Yamantaka, and the peaceful and wrathful deities.

In the Water Pig Year, many of those same artisans made images of the Sixteen Arhats from gold and copper. Using more than seven hundred *sang* of silver, Chökyi Gyalpo then built a statue of Könchok Trinley Sangpo, of greater than life size, called Meaningful to Behold. Chökyi Gyalpo's monks, led by Epa Norbu Chöpel, fashioned representations of the Buddha's fifteen miracles at Shravasti out of ground gems and powdered silk and built rock caves to shelter the images of the arhats. The miracle representations were placed in the chapel called Ogmin, and the arhats were placed in the chapel called Deden. They were repeatedly consecrated with the practice of an ocean of tantras.

In the thirteenth *rabjung*, in the Fire Horse Year, the unfinished work of Lujin was begun again by some wealthy monks led by Epa Gyaltsen. Then, accompanied by the scattering of auspicious flowers, the tulku of Könchok Trinley Sangpo was enthroned on the lion throne at the great seat, Jangchub Ling.

At Trolung, Chökyi Gyalpo established a tradition of the dances of the Dharma protectors, adding those of Beng Mahakala, Tsering Chen-nga, Vaishravana, and so forth. By the end of that year, the carvings of the twelve deeds were completed.

When Könchok Trinley Sangpo was alive, he had repeatedly said that it would be good to build a model of the Chakrasamvara mandala of sixty-two deities. In order to fulfill this intention, and to provide a crucial support for the practice of that meditation, Chökyi Gyalpo constructed that mandala—both its outer form and inner contents—in astonishing detail. The artisans he employed were the same as before. The mandala was completed in the Dragon Year and was placed in the Ngönga chapel and consecrated.

In the Earth Snake Year, the mahapandita Situ Chökyi Jungne came to visit Chökyi Gyalpo, and they exchanged many teachings and empowerments. In the Horse Year, Chökyi Gyalpo became seriously ill but soon recovered.

At Trolung monastery, the great accomplishment ceremony of Tsogu was performed on the twenty-ninth day of the sixth month of each year to fulfill the intention of Könchok Trinley Sangpo. On these occasions, Chökyi Gyalpo made vast offerings to the assembly of monks. In the second month of the Water Monkey Year, many Tibetan and Nepalese artisans, joined later by Dhanoshing, began to gather to construct images of the lineage lamas of Drikung, beginning with Vajradhara and including yidams and Dharma protectors, all of life size and made from gold and copper. These were completed in the Water Bird Year and were placed in the Chökor Dorje Nyingpo chapel. Then, using gold and silver, Chökyi Gyalpo built a Descending From the God Realm Stupa and a Lotus Heap Stupa. He also built an Auspicious Stupa of Many Doors, a little higher than the others, which contained the sixty-two deities of Chakrasamvara. For reasons of auspiciousness, he then built a Completely Victorious Stupa instead of a Parinirvana Stupa. To the right and left of the temple's main statue were placed images of Amitabha and the All-seeing Lord. The main statue stood two stories high, and the flanking images stood at a height of a little more than a story each. Their thrones and back supports were also made of gold and silver.

In the third month of the Wood Dog Year, all of this was completed without obstacle. From Lhasa, Chökyi Gyalpo then brought a complete set of the Kangyur and the *Tengyur*, and from Derge he brought two sets of the Kangyur printed in a special red ink. He then quickly fashioned images of the Thirty-five Buddhas

out of red and white sandalwood, along with a representation of the buddhafield of Dewachen. One by
one, he opened the mandalas—from both the old and
the new traditions—of the Three Roots, the wrathful
and peaceful deities, Yamantaka, Chakrasamvara, and
so forth, and these were consecrated many times with
auspicious prayers in gatherings led by the father and
son. When the artisans had finished their work, Chökyi
Gyalpo pleased them with many gifts. Each of the six
chapels was adorned with canopies and wall-hang-
ings, all as colorful and bright as if they had come from
the treasury of the emperor of China. The images
were dressed in excellent clothes and scarves. Marvelous butterlamps were brought in countless numbers
from China, Hor, Kashmir, and other places. In brief,
many inconceivably wonderful varieties of offering
materials were made and taken there.

Thus, Chökyi Gyalpo accomplished all that he had
intended. When he had completed his benefit of
beings in that life, many inauspicious signs were
observed. He gave extensive advice to all his follow-
ers, including the tulku of Könchok Trinley Sangpo,
saying especially that if it were not possible for them
to build his stupa in gold and silver, they should build
many stupas of various sizes in the upper and lower
parts of Drikung valley and divide his relics among
them. This, he said, would provide many causes for

the spread of the Dharma. Then, pointing to a lotus in a representation of Dewachen, he said: "I will be sitting here. Because I have prayed with one-pointed mind, there is no doubt that I will be born in Dewachen."

Then, although no particular disease had been diagnosed, Chökyi Gyalpo's health began to fail. On the twenty-first day of the month of Saga Dawa in his fifty-first year, as the first warmth of the morning sun struck the ground, his profound mind dissolved into the dharmadhatu, and the area was filled with rainbows and the sounds of music. Many other marvelous signs occurred. On the twenty-ninth day, Chökyi Gyalpo's holy remains were cremated in a large gathering and Yamantaka ceremony led by the supreme emanation Tendzin Drodul, the tulku of Könchok Trinley Sangpo.

On the forty-ninth day following the parinirvana, a stupa called One Hundred Thousand Relics was built during a special ceremony at Trolung. At the end of that year, ceremonies were also held in Tsewa, and following that, in the Wood Pig Year, a large image of Chökyi Gyalpo made of gold and silver was placed in the hall at Trolung. A large silver stupa, more than two stories high, was built at the great seat, Drikung Thil. A golden stupa was also built at Kailash. All this was done in accordance with custom.

Chökyi Gyalpo's successor was the peerless precious Dharma Lord Tendzin Drodul, and his chief disciple was Gartrul Könchok Tendzin Chökyi Nyima, who held the vast and profound teachings of the Drikung Kagyu that ripen and free. When Lord Jigten Sumgön appeared as the tathagata Lurik Drön, Gartrul was born as the youngest prince. At the time of Lord Jigten Sumgön himself, he appeared as Gar Chödingpa Shakya Pel, a principal disciple. At the time of the Victorious Ratna, he appeared as Ngawang Döndrub, a lama of Tsang. At the time of the peerless Chögyal Phuntsok, he appeared as Tendzin Phuntsok. At the time of Dharmakirti, he was called Tendzin Drakpa. Thus, he has been recognized as the reincarnation of many great beings.

Gartrul Rinpoche was born in Nangchen. From Chökyi Gyalpo he received, in succession, the vows of an upasaka, of a novice monk, and of full ordination. He received the complete teachings of the Drikung Kagyu and all knowledge contained in the sutras and tantras. He attended the lords Tendzin Drodul and Hlotrul Chökyi Gyatso, mastered all their teachings, and gained direct realization. In each moment, he was unstained by the eight worldly concerns. Later, he became the vajra master of Chökyi Nyima, the incarnation of Chökyi Gyalpo, and gave him all the teachings of the Drikung Kagyu, including instructions on the Eight Herukas. Thus, he showed inconceivable great kindness to this Dharma lineage.

There were also many others who perfected the two stages.

# Notes

1. Lord Jigten Sumgön (1143–1217), the founder of the Drikung Kagyu lineage.

2. Könchok Trinley Sangpo (1656–1718), the Second Drikung Kyabgön Chetsang Rinpoche.

3. Religious and secular.

4. The conditions supportive of Dharma practice, including birth as a human with complete sense faculties at a time and in a place where the Dharma is taught.

5. "The others in its group" refers to all other drinks containing alcohol.

6. This refers to the story of the rabbit who, on hearing an unfamiliar sound, perceived it as a threat and became afraid for no reason.

7. In religious practice.

8. Literally, "an ornament for the eyes."

9. A kind of one-legged spirit, sometimes invoked by gamblers.

10. Divination and shamanism.

11. Referring to one's own accomplishment of the path.

12. Meaning something that needs to be protected at both ends (in other words, by teacher and student together). The author is saying here that one needs to take full responsibility oneself for protecting the commitments of the path.

13. The higher tantric activities of engaging in sexual union and taking the lives of beings in order to liberate their mindstream.

14. This is the first of the actual "hundred teachings," numbered 1–103 in the Tibetan text.

15. Meaning something that appears cool on the surface, but that burns and is hot underneath.

16. Meaning a heartfelt disgust and turning away from the futility of samsara.

17. In the same way that a bird must finally land and join its shadow on the ground, each of us must finally die and experience the results of our karma.

18. This refers to the contentment of simplicity, free from grasping at objects of desire.

19. This refers to the careless or improper use of meat or of offerings made to the Three Jewels and to any use at all of wealth acquired in nonvirtuous ways.

20. The qualities of enlightenment.

21. A poetic metaphor for the earth in its role as foundation and support.

22. Special thanks to Wilson Hurley of the Mahayana Sutra and Tantra Center for suggesting this translation of the term *mchod.sdong* ("shrine, imbued with sacred power").

23. The physical attributes and marks traditionally associated with buddhahood.

24. A poetic metaphor for a rainbow.

25. "Pride" refers here to confidence in one's own awakened nature.

26. Obstructing spirits.

27. Like a snake in a bamboo tube, a samaya holder can go in only one direction: "up" towards enlightenment or "down" towards intensified confusion.

28. Naked mind, free from grasping and fixation.

29. A famous physician at the time of the Buddha.

30. A realm, still within samsara, in which beings are formless because of their high level of meditative stabilization.

31. The cessation of suffering as an experience sought for one's own benefit alone.

32. The various phenomena that arise as a result of one's practice. Clairvoyance is given here as an example.

33. Apparent indications of progress on the path.

34. For example, mind may be said to be "like space," but it is not space itself.

# GLOSSARY OF ENUMERATIONS

Two Accumulations: Merit and wisdom.

Two Kinds of Form Body: Nirmanakaya and sambhogakaya (see entry for three kayas).

Two Obscurations: Obscurations of the afflicting emotions and obscurations of knowledge.

Two Stages: The generation stage of tantric practice, wherein one visualizes oneself as a deity, and the completion stage, wherein one dissolves that visualization and rests the mind in formless contemplation.

Three Jewels: Buddha, Dharma, and Sangha.

Three Kinds of Morality: Avoiding nonvirtue, accumulating virtue, benefiting beings.

Three Kinds of Perseverance: The armor-like perseverance, the perseverance of action, and the perseverance that is not satisfied with what has already been accomplished.

Three Kayas: The three "bodies," or modes of being, of a buddha (the dharmakaya, "truth body"; sambhogakaya, "enjoyment body"; and nirmanakaya, "emanation body").

Three Lower Realms: The realms of hell beings, of hungry ghosts, and of animals.

Three Roots: The lamas (the root of blessings), the yidams (the root of attainments), and the Dharma protectors (the root of enlightened activity).

Three Secrets: The unceasing and indestructible realities of a buddha's body, speech, and mind.

Three Streams of Practice: Performing prostrations, reciting sutras, and dedicating merit.

Three Syllables: OM, AH, HUM.

Three Times: Past, present, and future.

Three Trainings: Discipline, meditation, and wisdom.

Three Vows: The vows of individual liberation (see entry for pratimoksha), of the mahayana, and of the vajrayana.

Three Ways of Pleasing: Pleasing one's teacher through respect and service, by offering necessities, and by practicing according to the teacher's instructions.

Three Worlds: The world of gods, the world of humans, and the world of nagas (water-dwelling serpent beings).

Four Characteristics: Phenomena are nonexistent, potent, apprehendable by the senses, and interdependent.

Four Empowerments: Vase empowerment, secret empowerment, wisdom empowerment, sacred word empowerment.

Four Kayas: The three kayas, plus the svabhavakakaya, representing their inseparable unity.

Four Obscurations: Obscurations of karma, obscurations of the afflicting emotions, obscurations of knowledge, and obscurations of habitual tendencies.

Four Powers, Confession of: A purification practice incorporating the generation of remorse over a misdeed, the determination never to repeat the misdeed, the antidote of practice (usually the generation of bodhicitta and recitation of mantra), and reliance on refuge in the Three Jewels.

Four Preliminaries: Classified in two sets of four each as "ordinary" and "extraordinary," these are (1) the contemplations on the precious human birth, impermanence, cause and effect, and the sufferings of samsara, and (2) the practices of refuge and prostrations, Vajrasattva mantra, mandala offerings, and guru yoga.

Five Paths: The sequential paths along which the bodhisattva progresses towards enlightenment: the path of accumulation, the path of preparation, the path of insight, the path of meditation, and the path of perfection (or no more learning).

Five Poisons: Desire, hatred, ignorance, arrogance, and jealousy.

Six Dharmas: The Six Yogas of Naropa (the practices of tummo, the illusory body, the dream state, luminosity, phowa, and bardo.)

Six Objects: The objects of perception of the six senses, including mind.

Seven Characteristics: The dharmakaya pervades all phenomena; it is the unification of supreme all-pervading emptiness and nonobjectified great compassion; it is great bliss, completely free from all suffering; it is inherently nonexistent and free from elaboration in its mode of abiding; it is the great embodiment of full compassion, unchanging from coemergent wisdom; it never varies from all the qualities described above and is free from coming, going, increasing, or decreasing; it is unceasing and not "just nothing"—instead, it is the embodiment of the ultimate great bliss.

Eight Worldly Concerns: Gain and loss, pleasure and pain, praise and blame, fame and disgrace.

Ten Bhumis: The ten levels, or stages, of a bodhisattva's progress on the path to full enlightenment.

Ten Virtuous Activities: In this context, these refer to copying Dharma texts, making offerings to Dharma texts, distributing copies of Dharma texts, giving teachings, reciting prayers, receiving teachings, reading, memorizing, contemplating, and meditating.

Twelve Deeds of the Buddha: The major themes in the life of Shakyamuni Buddha (descending from the Tushita heaven, entering the womb, taking birth, developing proficiency in the arts, enjoying the kingdom, renouncing the kingdom, undergoing austerities, going to Bodhgaya, subjugating the maras, attaining enlightenment, turning the wheel of Dharma, and attaining parinirvana).

# The Jewel Treasury of Advice

# Glossary of Terms

(Note: The definitions given here are not exhaustive and are meant only to provide access to these terms at the level of introductory study.)

Alaya: A foundational aspect of mind that can hold the seeds of dualistic thought or blossom into wisdom.

Bardo: The intermediate state through which consciousness passes between death and rebirth.

Bhumis: The levels, or stages, of accomplishment of a bodhisattva on the path to full enlightenment.

Bodhicitta: The "mind of enlightenment," the intention to accomplish full awakening for the benefit of all beings.

Bodhisattva: One who possesses bodhicitta and who works tirelessly for the spiritual welfare of others.

Buddha: Any fully enlightened being (one who has fully awakened all wisdom and fully purified all

obscurations), but referring especially to
Shakyamuni Buddha, the first of the Three Jewels
of Refuge.

Chöppön: One who prepares and arranges offerings
during the performance of tantric ritual.

Dharma: "Virtue and peace." The teachings of the
Buddha with regard both to what is taught and
what is experienced.

Dharmadhatu: All-encompassing space.

Dharmakaya: One of the three "bodies" of a buddha,
corresponding to enlightenment itself.

Dharmata: The essential nature of reality.

Drikung Kagyu: The branch of the Kagyu tradition
founded by Lord Jigten Sumgön (1143–1217) and
descending originally from the Indian siddhas
Tilopa and Naropa to the Tibetan masters Marpa,
Milarepa, Gampopa, and Phagmo Drupa, Lord
Jigten Sumgön's teacher.

Drönyer: A monastic official responsible for hospital-
ity and public relations.

Dzikyim: A rare, extraterrestrial metal.

Garuda: A mythological bird that hatches fully grown,
symbolizing the awakened mind.

Kangyur: The collected scriptures of the Buddha's teachings.

Karma: "Cause and result," referring especially to the positive or negative activities of body, speech, and mind and to their corresponding fruition in one's own experience.

Khenpo: An abbot or senior teacher of a monastery or college.

Kyorpön: The senior teaching assistant of a monastery or college.

Lama: One qualified to act as a teacher, especially with regard to tantra, in the Tibetan tradition of Buddhism.

Loppön: The master of studies in a monastery.

Maha Aryas: Those who directly experience and abide in the wisdom of emptiness.

Mahapandita: A scholar in the Buddhist tradition who is highly learned in the "ten knowledges": theatrical performance, astrology, poetry, the use of synonyms, the use of meter in classical composition, logic, linguistics, medicine, the creative arts, and metaphysics.

Mahayana: The "greater" vehicle of Buddhist teaching and practice, which transcends exclusive concern for one's own spiritual accomplishment and takes as its purpose the liberation of all beings.

Mandala: The "palace" of a deity, arranged as a circular diagram or three-dimensional structure with symbolic components surrounding a central figure.

Mantra: "Mind protection." Sanskrit syllables or words uttered as sacred sound.

Maras: Forces, often personified as demons, that obstruct spiritual progress.

Nirvana: Liberation from compulsive rebirth in samsara.

Parinirvana: An honorific term for the passing away of a buddha.

Phowa: The practice of consciousness transference at the moment of death.

Pratimoksha: The vows of "individual liberation," corresponding to the various levels and kinds of monastic ordination.

Rabjung: A sixty-year cycle according to the Tibetan calendar.

Sadhana: A tantric ritual and its corresponding text.

Samadhi: Meditative absorption.

Samaya: The vows of commitment in the practice of Buddhist tantra.

Samsara: Confused existence, which takes the form of cyclic rebirth in one or another of six realms, each of which is pervaded with suffering.

Sang: A unit of monetary value.

Sangha: The monastic and lay communities of those who follow the Buddha's teachings.

Shravakas: Those who take as their path the basic practices and teachings of Buddhism.

Siddhas: Highly accomplished practitioners of tantra.

Sojong: A ritual to purify and strengthen monastic vows.

Stupas: Structures, originally memorial mounds, whose form symbolizes the awakened mind and physical presence of the Buddha.

Sutras: Scriptures presenting the discourses of the Buddha.

Tantra: "Continuity," referring to the continuity of awakened mind and to the esoteric teachings and advanced meditation techniques that lead to enlightenment.

Tantrikas: Those who practice tantra.

Tathagata: "Thus Gone," an epithet for a buddha.

Tengyur: The collected scriptures of the teachings and commentaries of Indian Buddhist masters.

Terma: "Treasure," referring especially to teachings and symbolic objects concealed in the eighth or ninth centuries C.E. by Guru Padmasambhava and others and intended for discovery at a later time.

Thangkas: Scroll-mounted religious paintings in the Tibetan tradition.

Torma: Specially shaped and colored offering cakes or deity representations used in tantric ritual.

Tulku: The reincarnation of an accomplished lama.

Tummo: The practice of "inner heat," one of the Six Yogas of Naropa.

Upasaka: One who holds the vows of lay ordination: not to kill, steal, lie, take intoxicants, or engage in sexual misconduct.

Vajra Hell: The solidification of confusion and suffering that results from breaking one's samaya, misusing the power of tantra, or generating any other heavy negative karma.

Vajra Master: An accomplished practitioner and teacher of the vajrayana.

Vajra Recitation: The recitation of mantra.

Vajrayana: The diamond path, or "vehicle," of Buddhist tantra.

Vinaya: The vows of moral conduct of the Buddhist monastic tradition.

Yidam: A deity whose form and attributes embody a particular aspect of enlightenment and with whom the practitioner identifies in meditation.

# ABOUT THE TRANSLATOR

The village of Tsari and the area surrounding it is considered to be one of the most sacred places in Tibet. It was there that Khenpo Könchog Gyaltshen Rinpoche was born in the spring of 1946, and it was there that he spent his early years.

In 1959, because of the political situation in Tibet, Khenpo Rinpoche fled to India with his family. The family then settled in Darjeeling, where Rinpoche began his education. Even at a young age, he was an excellent and dedicated student, and he was able to complete his middle school studies in less than the average time.

At about this same time a new university, the Central Institute of Higher Tibetan Studies, opened in Varanasi, India. Determined to be among its first students, Khenpo Rinpoche traveled to Varanasi in October 1967 to seek admission. He then began a nine-year course of study that included Madhyamika,

Abhidharma, Vinaya, the *Abhisamayalankara*, and the *Uttaratantra*, as well as history, logic, and Tibetan grammar. In early 1968, he had the good fortune to take full monastic ordination from the great Kalu Rinpoche, and, shortly after graduating from the Institute, he received teachings from the Sixteenth Gyalwa Karmapa on the realization songs of the Indian mahasiddhas.

Even after completing this long and arduous course of study, Khenpo Rinpoche wanted only to deepen his knowledge and practice of the Dharma. With the same intensity that he brought to his earlier studies, Rinpoche sought out and received teachings and instructions from great Buddhist masters. One was the Venerable Khunu Lama Rinpoche, with whom Khenpo Rinpoche studied two works of Gampopa: *The Jewel Ornament of Liberation* and *The Precious Garland of the Excellent Path*. Rinpoche's studies with the Venerable Khunu Lama also included mahamudra and many of the songs of Milarepa.

Maintaining a balance between theoretical understanding and the practice of meditation, Khenpo Rinpoche began a three-year retreat in 1978 under the guidance of the enlightened master Khyunga Rinpoche. During this time, he was able to deepen and enhance his understanding of *The Fivefold Path of Mahamudra* and the profound *Gong Chik* text of Lord

Jigten Sumgön. He also received many other transmissions.

In 1982, the force of karma and the requests of many practitioners combined to bring Khenpo Rinpoche to the United States. Since that time, Rinpoche's compassion and dedication to the Dharma have taken him to all parts of the world. Rinpoche now travels tirelessly, giving teachings and organizing Dharma centers. He has translated all the major Drikung Kagyu meditation practices, and, because of his efforts, Western students are now able to read and perform the Chakrasamvara, Vajrayogini, Guru Yoga, Chöd, Green and White Tara, Chenrezik, Medicine Buddha, and other practices in their own language.

Wanting the teachings of Dharma to reach as many people as possible, Khenpo Rinpoche has quickly adapted himself to Western forms of communication. He has made appearances on television, been a guest on many radio programs, lectured extensively at colleges and universities, and spoken to the public through countless newspaper articles.

A skilled and dedicated translator, Rinpoche has published four books before this: *Prayer Flags, In Search of the Stainless Ambrosia, The Garland of Mahamudra Practices,* and *The Great Kagyu Masters.* A sixth book, a new translation of *The Jewel Ornament of Liberation,* is in production and will be released soon. In this way,

Rinpoche has been able to make important texts available to the public and to provide his students with a thorough and systematic training in the Dharma.

In 1985, Khenpo Rinpoche traveled to the main seat of the Drikung Kagyu lineage, Drikung Thil, in Tibet. There he was able to receive personal blessings, as well as instructions and transmissions of mahamudra and the Six Yogas of Naropa, from the enlightened master, the Venerable Pachung Rinpoche.

As a public figure, Khenpo Rinpoche continues to write, to translate texts, and to teach whenever requested. He recently returned from the Drikung Kagyu Institute in India, where he taught the *Gong Chik* to a group of about ninety monks and nuns. With the financial assistance of friends and students worldwide, Rinpoche was able to print 1,700 copies of the *Gong Chik* and to distribute them to the students of the Institute. In 1996, Rinpoche printed and distributed 1,500 copies of *Essence of the Mahayana Teachings* by Ngorje Repa, an important disciple of Lord Jigten Sumgön.

Remembering the struggles of his early years, Khenpo Rinpoche inspires and supports monks, nuns, and laypeople in their practice of the Dharma and is always ready to assist them in whatever way he can. To all, he gives of himself freely. With his heart and mind turned firmly towards the Dharma, he compassionately and with great patience shows the way.

# ABOUT THE EDITOR

Rick Finney, a long-time student of Buddhism and the Tibetan language, has worked closely with Khenpo Könchog Gyaltshen Rinpoche on many of his published works since 1982. Rick lives in Gaithersburg, Maryland, with his wife and children and is currently working toward a degree in East Asian Studies at the Elliott School of International Affairs of the George Washington University.

# The Jewel Treasury of Advice

# INDEX

# Index

Mantra 12, 17–19, 33–34, 42, 62, 79–80, 86, 88
Maras 29, 40, 44, 46, 61, 88
Milarepa 2, 59, 84, 92
Mindfulness 33, 46

## N

Nagarjuna 7

## O

Ordinary view 33, 47
Ordinary mind 37

## P

Panoramic awareness 36
Paramitas 5
Parinirvana 68, 70, 81, 86
Patience 5, 30, 94
Phowa 6, 41, 80, 86
Pratimoksha 28, 78, 86
Pride 16, 39, 75

## R

Rabjung 66, 86

## S

Sadhana 57, 60, 86
Samadhi 31, 86

Samaya 18, 32, 34, 75, 86, 88
Samsara 1, 6–7, 13–14, 19–20, 24–25, 31, 33, 35, 44, 46–47, 74, 76, 80, 86–87
Sangha 77, 87
Seven Characteristics 43, 45, 80
Shravakas 18, 39, 87
Siddhas 84, 87
Six Dharmas 41, 80
Six Objects 36, 37, 80
Sojong 61, 87
Stupas 65, 69, 87
Suffering 1–4, 20, 23–24, 35, 40, 76, 80, 87–88
Sutras 71, 78, 87

## T

Tantra 6–7, 42, 75, 85–88
Ten Bhumis 43, 81
Ten Virtuous Activities 58, 81
Tengyur 68, 87
Terdrom 54–55, 59–60
Terma 55–56, 88
Thangkas 59, 88
Three Jewels 17, 23, 27, 46, 49, 75, 77, 79, 84
Three Kayas 19, 44, 48, 77–79
Three Kinds of Morality 30, 77
Three Lower Realms 2, 24, 78
Three Roots 69, 78
Three Secrets 49
Three Streams of Practice 61, 78

# VAJRA PUBLICATIONS

VAJRA PUBLICATIONS is a nonprofit publisher on books on the Vajrayana Buddhist teachings of the Drikung Kagyu Lineage. In addition, we publish translations of Drikung sadhanas and prayers. If you would like to receive a copy of our mail order catalogue, or be kept informed about our future publications, please write or call us at:

*Tibetan Meditation Center*
**9301 Gambrill Park Rd.**
**Frederick, MD 21702**
**(301) 473-9220**

As a nonprofit publisher, Vajra Publications is dedicated to the publication of Dharma books for the benefit of all beings and for the preservation of the Drikung Kagyu lineage. We depend on sponsors in order to continue our translation and publishing projects. If you would like to make a donation or underwrite a specific publication to help us continue our Dharma work, or to receive information about opportunities for planned giving, please write to:
Gejong Palmo, editor-in-chief, at the above address.

Vajra Publications is a nonprofit, charitable 501 (c) (3) organization and an imprint of the Tibetan Meditation Center - Ratnashri Dharma Chakra; headquarters of the Drikung Kagyu lineage in north America.

*Please treat this book with respect as it contains the precious teachings of the Dharma. It should not be placed on the floor or stepped over, nor should other objects be placed on top of it.*